Published by
Princeton Architectural Press
37 East Seventh Street
New York, NY 10003

For a catalog of books published by Princeton Architectural Press, call toll free 800.722.6657
or visit www.papress.com

Copyright © 1999 Princeton Architectural Press
All photographs copyright © Esto Photographics, Inc.
03 02 01 00 99   5 4 3 2 1   First Edition

Editor & book design: Mark Lamster
Jacket design: Sara E. Stemen
Drawings: Jonah Pregerson & Mark Watanabe

Acknowledgments
I would like to thank my colleagues at Esto Photographics, especially Kent Draper and
Laura Bolli; Mary Doyle and Mike Kimines of TSI for their help in preparing these images;
and Mark Lamster for his support from start to finish—Erica Stoller

Princeton Architectural Press acknowledges Bernd-Christian Döll, Jane Garvie, Caroline
Green, Leslie Ann Kent, Clare Jacobson, Therese Kelly, and Annie Nitschke
—Kevin C. Lippert, publisher

For the licensing of Ezra Stoller images, contact Esto Photographics.
Fine art reproductions of Stoller prints are available through the James Danziger Gallery.

Printed in China

Library of Congress Cataloging-in-Publication Data
The Chapel at Ronchamp / photographs by Ezra Stoller ;
   introduction by Eugenia Bell. -- 1st ed.
      p.   cm. -- (The Building Blocks series)
   Includes bibliographical references.
   ISBN 1-56898-184-8 (alk. paper)
   1. Notre-Dame-du-Haut (Chapel : Ronchamp, France)
   2. Le Corbusier, 1887–1965 Criticism and interpretation.
   3. Ronchamp (France).--Buildings, structures, etc.   I. Stoller, Ezra.
   II. Series: Building blocks series (New York, N.Y.)
   NA5551.R55 C48   1999
   779'.44453--dc21   98-54679
                                             CIP

The Chapel at Ronchamp

Photographs by Ezra Stoller

Introduction by Eugenia Bell

building blocks

Princeton Architectural Press • New York

The BUILDING BLOCKS series presents the masterworks of modern architecture through the iconic images of acclaimed architectural photographer Ezra Stoller.

Contents

Preface

Ezra Stoller

I ARRIVED IN PARIS in 1955 with several assignments to be covered, two of which were for important religious buildings. The first of these, for the now defunct *Holiday* magazine, was the great cathedral at Chartres; the other was Le Corbusier's Chapel at Ronchamp, a commission from the Museum of Modern Art in New York. I immediately drove out to Chartres to scout the cathedral and, despite all the brainwashing, was disappointed by some things about it, though I did think I could get some good pictures.

It had been my practice when assigned to photograph a building to inform the architect and to get the names of people on the job who could be helpful to me. Back in Paris, I phoned Le Corbusier's office and was told that he would cooperate with me only if the museum would purchase two of his paintings. I tried to explain that I had no influence with the museum but didn't get anywhere. I expect that Le Corbusier had numerous photographers in tow and that one more

meant nothing to him. But having come all the way to France, I couldn't very well leave without any pictures, so I decided to go out to Ronchamp on my own.

As luck would have it, there was a gentleman there who spoke English pretty well and offered to help me with the logistics of the shoot—finding a place to stay and the like. Aside from that man, hardly anybody came by in the two or three days I was photographing there except for a group of priests. They were friendly, and some posed in the photographs.

Ronchamp was a difficult assignment, especially on the interior, which was quite dark and had no electrical power. Film doesn't have the range of sensitivity of the human eye, so normally you light up the shadow areas to give a sense of what's happening. But at Ronchamp the minute you added light you changed the character of the space. Maintaining detail in both the stained-glass windows and in the wall of the nave was particularly trying.

The upshot of this story is that I was so carried away by the chapel, which is essentially a modest building, that I used up all my film and never did get back to Chartres.

Introduction

Eugenia Bell

PERCHED ON A HILL a few miles from the Swiss border in the Haute-Saône region of eastern France, the white mirage of Le Corbusier's Chapel of Notre-Dame-du-Haut hovers above the village of Ronchamp. A pilgrimage site since the thirteenth century, the building now receives as many students of architecture as worshippers of the Virgin Mary, to whom it is dedicated. The building's peaceful hilltop setting belies a controversial history. Though it is now considered one of the masterpieces of modern architecture and a landmark work in Le Corbusier's formidable *oeuvre*, the project very nearly did not come to pass. Years after its completion, with wounds still healing, the parish's longtime chaplain Abbé René Bolle-Reddat averred that "someone some day will be able to write about the problems that this chapel experienced at the time of its birth, the struggles that had to be undertaken on all fronts, in what humus, nauseating at times, this flower of grace arose."[1]

The courting of Le Corbusier (born Charles-Edouard Jeanneret in 1887) began in early 1950, when the task of rebuilding what remained of the war-wrecked chapel on Bourlémont hill was designated to La Société Immoblière (development corporation) de Notre-Dame-du-Haut. The corporation's original intention was to restore what remained of the existing chapel, which had been destroyed by German bombing in 1944. That building too was a replacement—the previous chapel had burned in a lightning-induced fire in 1913. After reviewing the costs of restoration, however, it became clear to members of the corporation that complete reconstruction was a more sound decision. In need of an architect, the group turned to the Commission d'Art Sacré, the body of the French Church that made such recommendations, and specifically to two local members of the commission—Canon Ledeur of Besançon (the commission's secretary) and François Mathey—for suggestions on whom best to solicit for the new design. There was little question in their minds as to who they should nominate: Le Corbusier.

Skeptical about a project for the Catholic Church, Le Corbusier, who was raised a Protestant, initially refused the offer to submit drawings for the chapel. Just a few months earlier, his design for a subterranean basilica at Sainte-Baume had been rejected, and it was no secret that the architect remained bitter about what he perceived as the church's lack of vision. But his interest was peaked upon learning more about Ronchamp. The hilltop had been home to a third-century B.C. pagan temple and a number of different structures dating as far back as the fourteenth century A.D., when church records reveal worshippers first flocking to the site. Informed of the sanctity of the spot, Le Corbusier made his first visit to Ronchamp in June of 1950. After many hours spent walking and sketching the hillside, the concept of building on the significant site became more and more appealing, and the architect began to reconsider the idea of working for the church.

It was undoubtedly the support and friendship of Ledeur, Mathey, and their colleague clergyman Pierre Marie Alain Couturier that led Le Corbusier to accept the commission and allowed him to carry out the controversial design. All three were leaders of a movement that aimed to revive the French Church through the application of contemporary art and architecture. Working together on the Commission d'Art Sacré, they demonstrated their commitment through the publication of the journal *L'Art Sacré* and, more importantly, through their support of Europe's leading artists, regardless of their faith. All felt that the religious context was ideally suited to contemporary trends in the arts and were committed to the belief that the integrity of artistic expression takes precedence over an artist's religious piety. Couturier, for example, was responsible for commissioning Pierre Bonnard, Marc Chagall, and Fernand Léger to embellish Notre-Dame-de-Toute-Grace in Assy with their paintings, and participated in the hiring of Henri Matisse to create a decorative program for the Chapel at Vence. Together, the trio offered Le Corbusier the unheard of license to "go all the way" at Ronchamp, with "free rein to create what you will."[2] Not surprisingly, Le Corbusier found it impossible to refuse such an offer. Sadly, Couturier died before he could see the completion of the chapel (or Le Corbusier's later monastery, La Tourette, of 1955 at Lyons).

A native son of the neighboring Jura Mountains in Switzerland, Le Corbusier, in the words of Ledour, "forged an immediate bond with the landscape" upon his first visit to the site.[3] The commission left him with a singular opportunity to manifest his belief in the integral relationship between architecture and nature, and nature and religious experience. His career and reputation established, the decision to accept the job was also in keeping with a resolution to only take on work with a personal resonance. The project at Ronchamp satisfied the architect on all counts.

Le Corbusier's bell-shaped plan for the chapel was conceived in a series of rapidly drawn sketches made on that first June trip, and was driven by his response to the site: "One begins with the acoustic of the landscape," he wrote, "taking as a starting point the four horizons. These are, the plain of the Saône, opposite to it the hills of Alsace, and on the other sides two valleys. The design is conceived in conformity with these horizons—in acceptance of them."[4]

From the outset, Le Corbusier's intentions were metaphysical rather than religious, his desire to create a lyrical, plastic space to serve as "a vessel of intense concentration and meditation." Toward this end, the building was constructed of walls of sprayed untreated concrete (*béton brut* or gunnite) and whitewashed with a coat of plaster to leave a rough surface. "The whiteness of lime is absolute," the architect claimed, "everything frees itself from it, inscribes itself on it, black on white: it is frank and loyal." In fact, the use of concrete was as much a pragmatic decision as an aesthetic one: Le Corbusier recognized the difficulty of transporting more bulky materials up the hillside and the consequent fact that he would "have to put up with sand and cement."[5]

The chapel's sweeping, earthen-colored roof—composed of a pair of parallel 6 centimeter concrete shells—contrasts in both color and texture (the formwork is still visible on the smooth surface) with the coarse, bright-white walls. Likened to everything from a nun's habit to a ship's prow, the form of the roof was consciously designed by the architect with a crab's shell in mind. Like other coverings in Le Corbusier's *oeuvre*, the load is not carried by the walls themselves, as it appears to be, but by sixteen pillars embedded in the north and south walls.

The building's two principal facades orient toward the south and the east, and are separated by a pinched wall that swiftly rises as it moves toward the corner. The south facade, with its gently sloping

wall punctured by a series of openings for stained glass, holds the chapel's main entrance. Ranging in shape from small slots to deep recesses, the windows reflect the depth of the wall and create a mosaic of light on the interior. Le Corbusier's determination to employ this design element is apparent in his earliest conceptual sketches, which show a plethora of openings in a variety of sizes and shapes. Following protests from the parish, however, the final design became far more ordered and restrained. Adjacent to the wall, a two-ton, enameled steel door in primary colors bears the abstracted image of a giant open hand, at once a welcoming and a blessing to those entering the chapel.

Though the architect claimed that the "requirements of religion have had little effect on the design," the eastern facade was specifically created to accommodate an outdoor chapel for ten-thousand worshippers, the focal point of the thrice yearly, formally planned pilgrimage masses at the hilltop.[6] The scale of this exterior space gives an impression of grandness, exercising a gravitational pull toward the altar. Le Corbusier originally intended to enclose this space with a large semi-circular concrete band, a proposal that was wisely dropped. Instead, a series of landmarks—including a ziggurat of rubble (which serves as a monument to the region's war dead) from the previous, bombed-out chapel—defines the perimeter of this outdoor space.

The west facade, the only blind facade on the building, features a double-barrel gutter that runs rainwater into a receiving pool opposite the building at ground level (rain-collection was part of the program given to the architect by the parish). The rain pool contains three pyramids and a cylinder, all in *béton brut*—a sculptural composition vaguely reminiscent of Le Corbusier's roof garden for the Marseilles Unité d'Habitation (1947–53). These geometrical elements provide textural and formal contrast to the gentle bulge of the outside wall of the chapel's confessional. The west facade curves around to the

north, where a pair of towers stand in resolute opposition, separated by the visitors' entrance.

Upon entering the chapel, the play of intermittent light beckons one to explore. Light pierces through the south wall into the darkened space. Punched through this thick membrane, clear windows offer a blurred view of the landscape beyond, painted panes playfully tribute the Virgin Mary, and colored glass filters light throughout the central space in a muted, otherworldly fashion. Le Corbusier relieved the weight of the roof on the interior by separating the south and east walls from the ceiling with a narrow strip of light. The floor follows the natural slope of the hillside leading down toward the altar, which is situated beneath the highest point in the chapel. Behind the altar, a three-hundred-year-old statue of the Virgin Mary sits in an illuminated window box, presiding over both the indoor and outdoor chapels. Three interior side chapels offer additional spaces for private services or meditation. All are placed in the bases of the chapel's periscope-like towers, and benefit from the dramatically filtered light that pours down the towers' shafts.

Le Corbusier conceived of Ronchamp as a three-dimensional work of sculpture to be viewed from all sides, and intended visitors to follow what he described as a "*promenade architecturale*" in order to capture a series of "*événements plastiques*" when approaching the building and entering its spaces. Of this poetic journey, he wrote:

Forms bathed in light. Inside and outside; below and above. Inside: we enter, we walk around, we look at things while walking around and the forms take on meaning; they expand, they combine with one another.

Unité d'Habitation, Marseille (1947–53). *Stoller's photograph of the Unité's roof terrace highlights the sculptural form of a fluted concrete ventilation shaft.*

Outside: we approach, we see, our interest is aroused, we stop, we appreciate, we turn around, we discover. We receive a series of sensory shocks, one after the other, varying in emotion: the *jeu* comes into play. We walk, we turn, we never stop moving or turning towards things. Note the tools we use to perceive architecture… the architectural sensation we experience stems from hundreds of different perceptions. It is the "*promenade*," the movements we make that act as the motor for architectural events.[7]

Le Corbusier's concept of architectural procession was clearly influenced by the architecture of the ancient Greeks, and particularly by the staging of the Parthenon on the Athenian Acropolis—the prototypical sanctuary atop a hill and the architect's interpretive model for Ronchamp. Indeed, throughout his architectural manifesto, *Towards a New Architecture* (*Vers une architecture*), Le Corbusier referred to the Parthenon and the Acropolis as architectural ideals. Beyond procession, from Greek architecture Le Corbusier absorbed the ancient system of proportion based on the Golden Section (and developed his own system of ideal measurement, the "Modulor"), which he regularly employed to order and balance his designs.

Ezra Stoller's photographs of the chapel provide a deeply sympathetic promenade around and through the building (though Le Corbusier's tour moved counterclockwise). Stoller arrived at the Chapel in 1955, the year the building was completed, on a commission from the Museum of Modern Art in New York, as the preeminent architectural photographer of the day. Revered by architects and magazine editors for his ability to produce iconic, factual images, Stoller's photographs—several of which are peopled by a group of visiting priests—also succeed at evoking the spirituality of the site.

The construction of Notre-Dame-du-Haut began in 1953, after the Besançon Commission d'Art Sacré approved a refined scheme for

Unité d'Habitation, Marseille. Some critics found it difficult to reconcile Le Corbusier's emphasis on "rational" planning and form at the Marseille Unité with the spiritual poetry of his chapel at Ronchamp.

the building. Even before it opened, the building and the architect were mercilessly attacked by critics, the church, and the citizens of Ronchamp. The chapel was many things to its critics: a highly irrational building, a step backward for the modern movement, a nod to archaic technology donned in modern appliqué. But supporters saw it as an example of plastic poetry modified by the architect's rationalism, a logical progression in the development of the modernist idiom, and a place of intense beauty and feeling—a bold return to the architect's spiritual roots.

Le Corbusier took on the chapel at a time when his reputation as an architect and theorist was assured, but when he had nonetheless failed to achieve his great ambition to humanistically transform modern living through architecture and urban planning. Though a few of his public housing projects—such as the Marseilles Unité, a veritable city within a building—were realized, these were isolated events, and did not amount to the cultural overhaul he sought. Indeed, his vision of the "Tower in the Park" would later be corrupted to disastrous effect in American public housing. As the architectural historian William Curtis has written, "it was almost as if the post-war world conspired to stop [Le Corbusier] from having a [societal] effect, leaving, presumably, the idiosyncratic poet of form to dig ever deeper into the private worlds of metaphor." A chapel was an ideal outlet for such a poet. "I have not experienced the miracle of faith," the architect wrote, "but I have often known the miracle of inexpressible space, the apotheosis of plastic emotion." As he wrote in *Towards a New Architecture*, his was the search for the "pure creation of the spirit."[8]

Le Corbusier attempted to convince members of the local parish and the citizens of Ronchamp that his intention was not to shock, that he was sympathetic to the Haute-Saône landscape, to their spiritual attachment to it, and to their faith. The public was not immediately receptive to his protestations. But the building slowly won them over.

Beginning in the late 1950s, the parish's chaplain began the intermittent publication of the *Journal de Notre-Dame-du-Haut*, filled with everything from marriages and death notices to politics to the travails of young American visitors to the chapel. Not an issue of the journal slipped by without mention of the revered architect—the November 1965 edition mourns Le Corbusier's death with the headline "*Une année terrible!*" As one leafs through issues of the journal, it becomes clear that the once hesitant and intimidated town, which had refused electricity and water to the building when it was first completed, has come to care deeply for it—and for its architect.

1. Introductory letter by Abbé René Bolle-Reddat, *Le Journal de Notre Dame du Haut* (December 1971): 4.

2. Le Corbusier, quoted in Danièle Pauly, *Le Corbusier: La Chapelle de Ronchamp* (Basel: Birkhäuser, 1987), 59.

3. Ibid., 60.

4. Le Corbusier, *Oeuvre complète, vol. 5: 1946–1952* (Zurich: Verlag für Architektur, 1953), 72.

5. Le Corbusier, quoted in William J. R. Curtis, *Modern Architecture Since 1900* (Oxford: Phaidon, 1982), 273; Le Corbusier, quoted in Maurice Besset, *Qui était Le Corbusier* (Geneva: Skira, 1968), 17.

6. Le Corbusier, *Oeuvre complète*, 72.

7. Le Corbusier, "Les tendances de l'architecture rationaliste en relation avec la peinture et la sculpture," *Architecture Vivante* 7 (1936): 7.

8. Curtis, *Modern Architecture*, 272; Le Corbusier, quoted in ibid., 273; Le Corbusier, *Towards a New Architecture*, trans. Frederick Etchells (New York: Dover, 1986), 203.

Plates

21

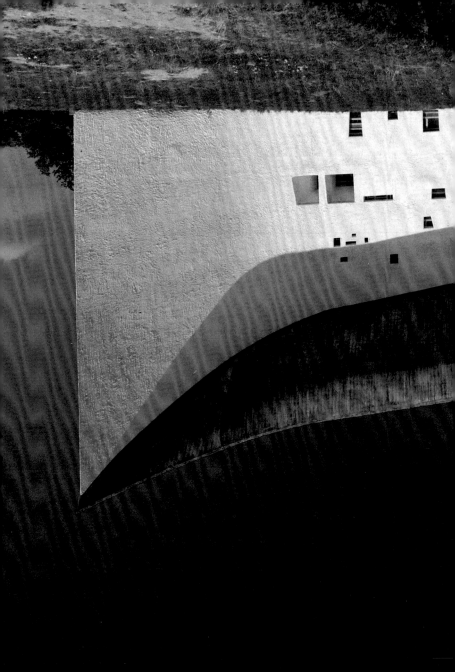

Drawings & Plans

0   50'   100'

1. CHAPEL 3. OUTDOOR CHAPEL 5. CARETAKER'S HOUSE

2. MEMORIAL PYRAMID 4. PILGRIMS' HOUSING 6. PATH TO SUMMIT

I. ALTAR	5. SOUTH SIDE CHAPEL	9. WEST SIDE CHAPEL
2. CHOIR	6. CONFESSIONALS	IO. EAST ENTRANCE
3. SACRISTY	7. EAST SIDE CHAPEL	II. EXTERIOR ALTAR &
4. MAIN ENTRANCE	8. NORTH ENTRANCE	PULPIT

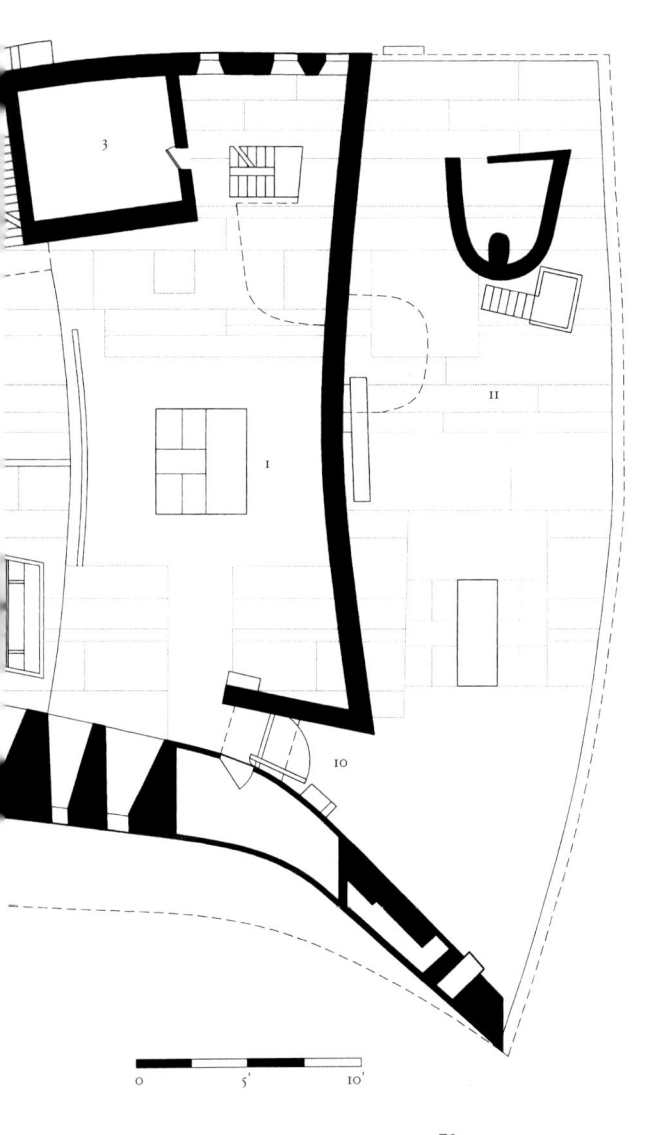

3

II

I

10

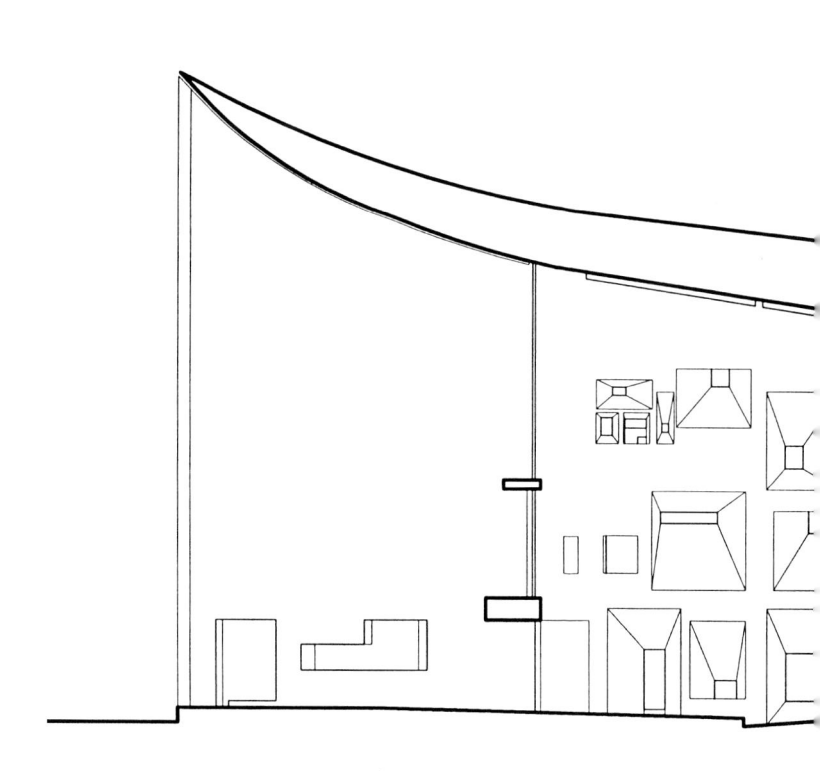

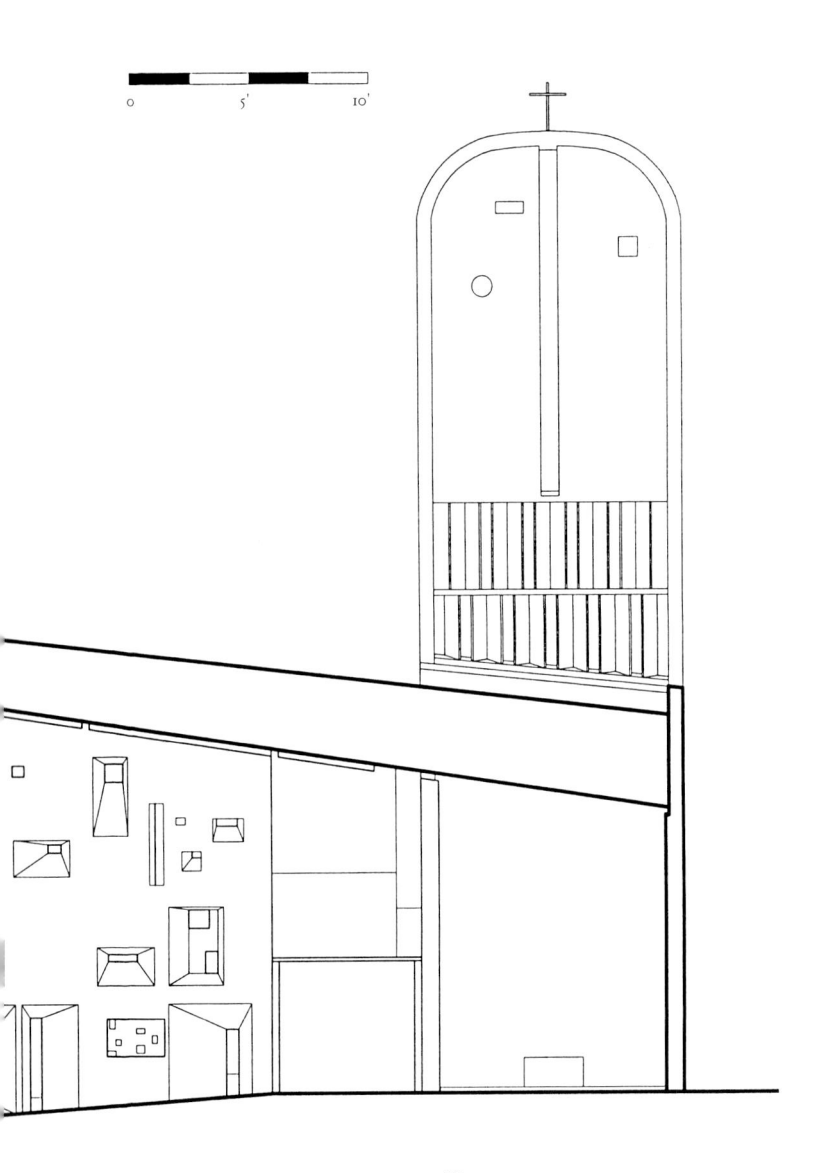

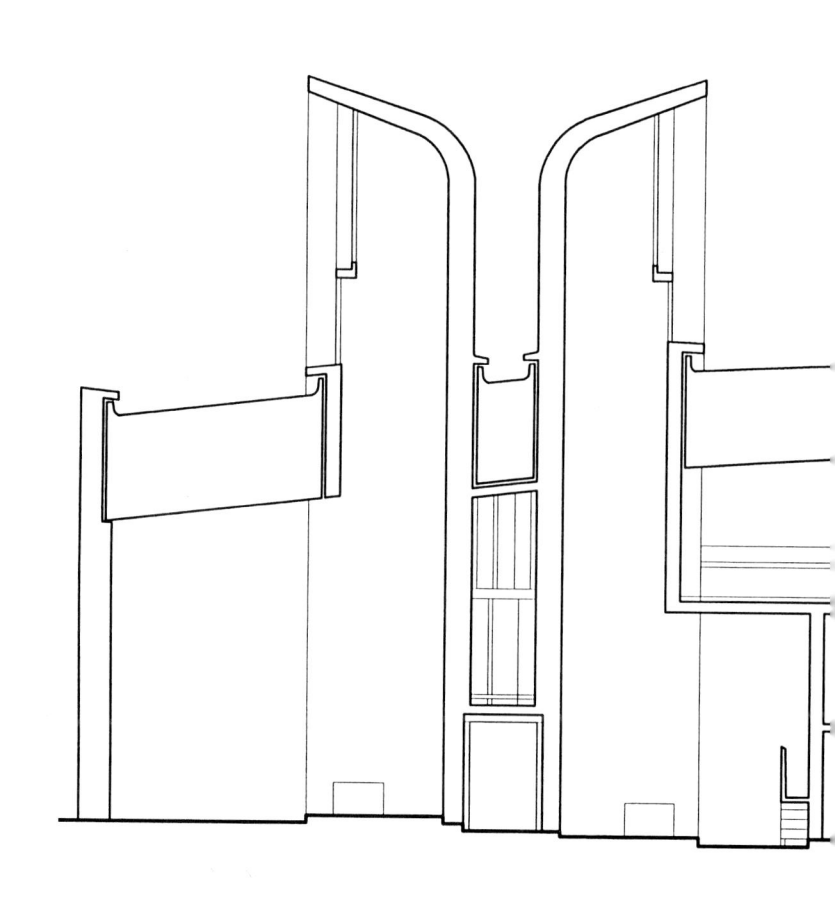

0　　　　　5'　　　　　10'

Key to Photographs

[*] *All photographs taken by Ezra Stoller in 1955.*